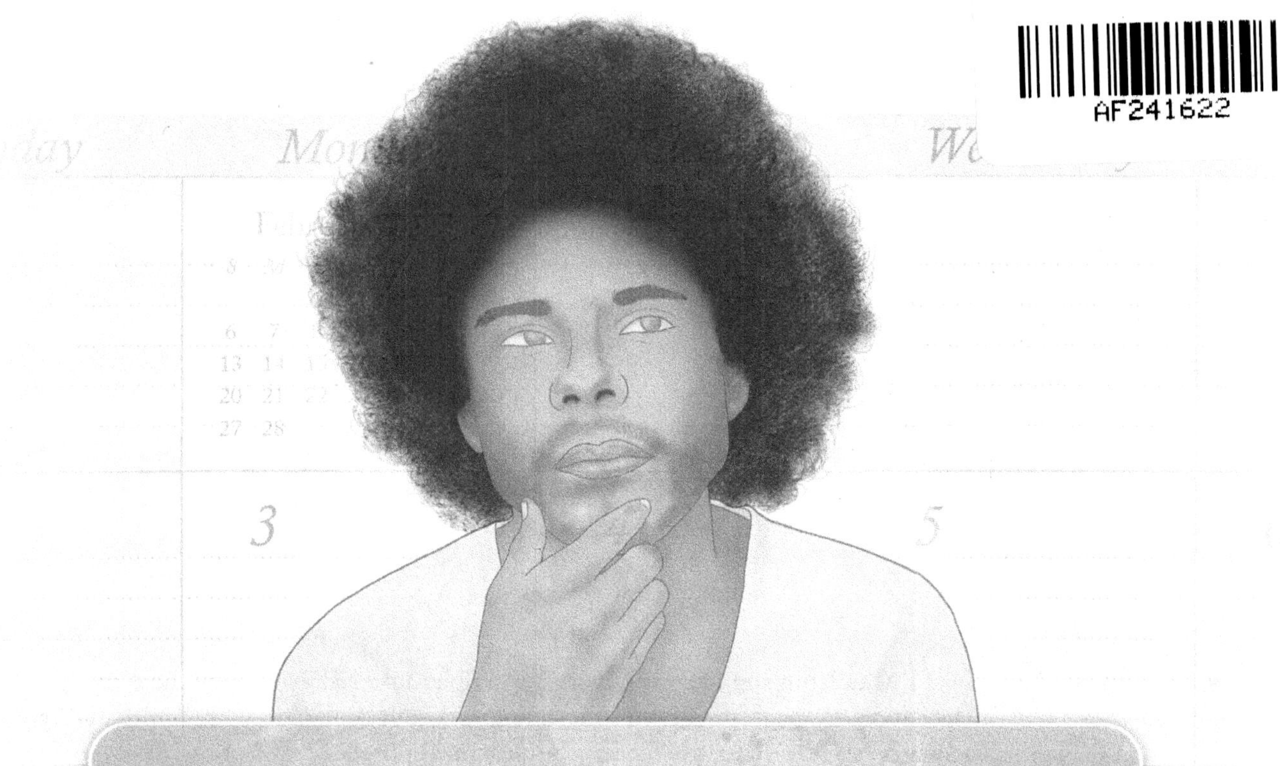

2022–2024 Monthly Planner

Colorable Three-Year Black History Calendar

By **Daniel J. Middleton**

UNIQUE Coloring

Layout and Design by Daniel J. Middleton
Associate Designer: Karen Dyer

First published in the United States
in November 2021 by Unique Coloring.
Printed by Ingram Book Group, LLC.

ISBN: 978-1-935702-50-4 (Paperback)

1 2 3 4 5 6 7 8 9 10   IBG   25 24 23 22 21

VISIT US ONLINE:
www.uniquecoloring.com

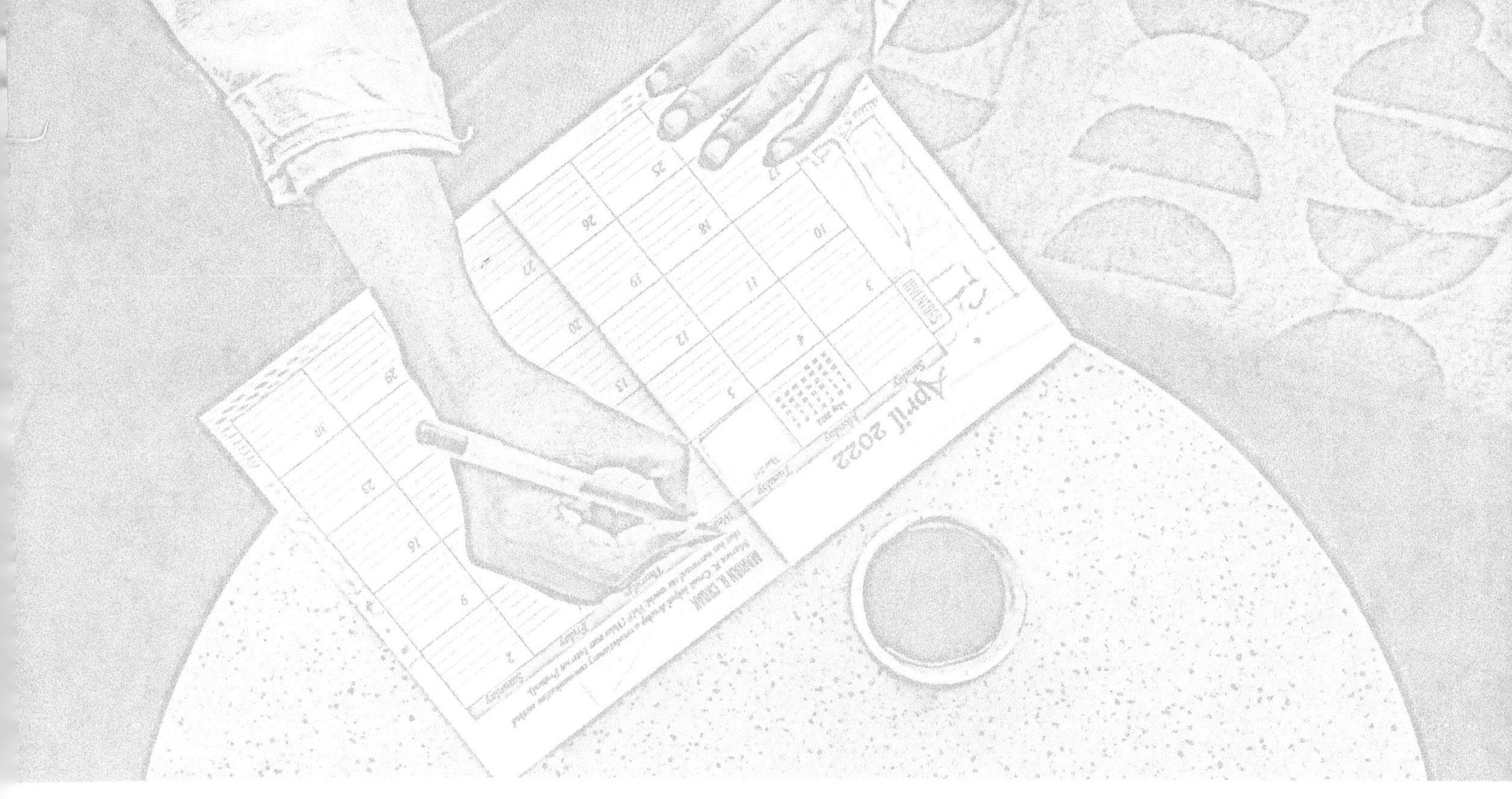

INTRODUCTION

Unlike other monthly planners on the market, this three-year calendar celebrates black achievement and features twelve prominent figures across three fields of experience. We opted for three years to allow for a long trajectory, so you can schedule events well into the future while focusing on pressing duties and short-term goals. And the planner's three-year structure won't leave you feeling overwhelmed.

It is up to you to tailor the planner to your needs, which is why you won't see days marked throughout, not even federal holidays. It is up to you to note days of importance and occasions you deem relevant. This planner is a time-management system designed to help you stay organized while keeping a healthy work-life balance. You are encouraged to use the 36 calendar months and their associated pages to write your general schedules and upcoming events. Actively engaging with the planner will help you remain committed and disciplined as you increase your level of productivity. And you won't forget the little things that demand your attention.

Happy organizing!

DANIEL J. MIDDLETON
Author & Illustrator

2021 AT A GLANCE

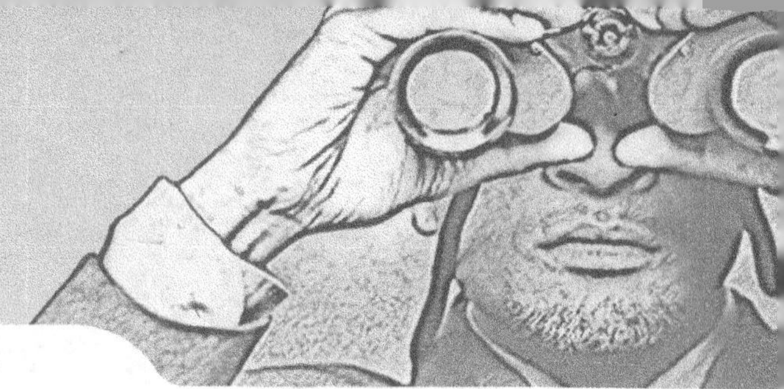

January 2021

S	M	T	W	T	F	S
					1	2
3	4	5	6	7	8	9
10	11	12	13	14	15	16
17	18	19	20	21	22	23
24	25	26	27	28	29	30
31						

February 2021

S	M	T	W	T	F	S
	1	2	3	4	5	6
7	8	9	10	11	12	13
14	15	16	17	18	19	20
21	22	23	24	25	26	27
28						

March 2021

S	M	T	W	T	F	S
	1	2	3	4	5	6
7	8	9	10	11	12	13
14	15	16	17	18	19	20
21	22	23	24	25	26	27
28	29	30	31			

April 2021

S	M	T	W	T	F	S
				1	2	3
4	5	6	7	8	9	10
11	12	13	14	15	16	17
18	19	20	21	22	23	24
25	26	27	28	29	30	

May 2021

S	M	T	W	T	F	S
						1
2	3	4	5	6	7	8
9	10	11	12	13	14	15
16	17	18	19	20	21	22
23	24	25	26	27	28	29
30	31					

June 2021

S	M	T	W	T	F	S
		1	2	3	4	5
6	7	8	9	10	11	12
13	14	15	16	17	18	19
20	21	22	23	24	25	26
27	28	29	30			

July 2021

S	M	T	W	T	F	S
				1	2	3
4	5	6	7	8	9	10
11	12	13	14	15	16	17
18	19	20	21	22	23	24
25	26	27	28	29	30	31

August 2021

S	M	T	W	T	F	S
1	2	3	4	5	6	7
8	9	10	11	12	13	14
15	16	17	18	19	20	21
22	23	24	25	26	27	28
29	30	31				

September 2021

S	M	T	W	T	F	S
			1	2	3	4
5	6	7	8	9	10	11
12	13	14	15	16	17	18
19	20	21	22	23	24	25
26	27	28	29	30		

October 2021

S	M	T	W	T	F	S
					1	2
3	4	5	6	7	8	9
10	11	12	13	14	15	16
17	18	19	20	21	22	23
24	25	26	27	28	29	30
31						

November 2021

S	M	T	W	T	F	S
	1	2	3	4	5	6
7	8	9	10	11	12	13
14	15	16	17	18	19	20
21	22	23	24	25	26	27
28	29	30				

December 2021

S	M	T	W	T	F	S
			1	2	3	4
5	6	7	8	9	10	11
12	13	14	15	16	17	18
19	20	21	22	23	24	25
26	27	28	29	30	31	

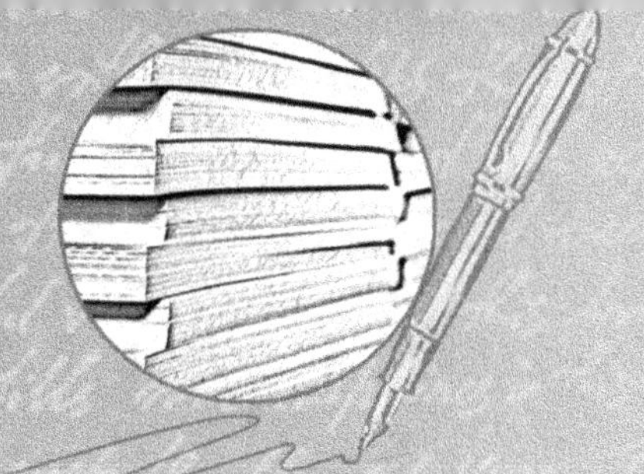

Descriptor	Detail

Descriptor	Detail

Descriptor	Detail

Descriptor	Detail

Descriptor	Detail

Descriptor	Detail

Other Important Items

Inventors 2022

"Unleash your creativity"

January 2022

Sunday	Monday	Tuesday

Post It!

February 2022

S	M	T	W	T	F	S
		1	2	3	4	5
6	7	8	9	10	11	12
13	14	15	16	17	18	19
20	21	22	23	24	25	26
27	28					

2	3	4
9	10	11
16	17	18
23	24	25
30	31	

FREDERICK MCKINLEY JONES

He revolutionized refrigerated transport by inventing the first portable air-cooling unit for trucks. He also co-founded Thermo King Corporation.

Wednesday	Thursday	Friday	Saturday
			1
5	6	7	8
12	13	14	15
19	20	21	22
26	27	28	29

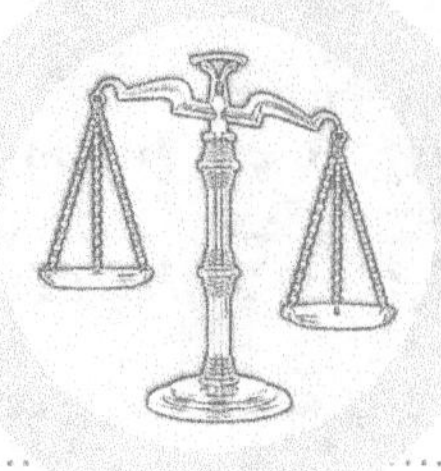

Work/LIFE Balance

Meetings

Appointments

Goals

Activities

Meetings

Appointments

Weekly *to-do* List

Monday

Tuesday

Wednesday

Thursday

Friday

Saturday

Sunday

February 2022

Sunday	Monday	Tuesday
		1
6	7	8
13	14	15
20	21	22
27	28	

FREDERICK MCKINLEY JONES

The frozen aisle at your local grocer remains stocked largely because of Frederick's cooling unit, which received a U.S. patent on July 12, 1940.

Wednesday	Thursday	Friday	Saturday
2	3	4	5
9	10	11	12
16	17	18	19
23	24	25	26

March 2022

S	M	T	W	T	F	S
		1	2	3	4	5
6	7	8	9	10	11	12
13	14	15	16	17	18	19
20	21	22	23	24	25	26
27	28	29	30	31		

Post It!

February 2022

Work/LIFE Balance

Meetings

Appointments

Goals

Activities

Meetings

Weekly *to-do* List

<table>
<tr><td>Monday</td><td></td></tr>
<tr><td>Tuesday</td><td>Saturday</td></tr>
<tr><td>Wednesday</td><td></td></tr>
<tr><td>Thursday</td><td>Sunday</td></tr>
<tr><td>Friday</td><td></td></tr>
</table>

March 2022

Sunday	Monday	Tuesday
		1
6	7	8
13	14	15
20	21	22
27	28	29

Learn more by scanning the QR code using the camera on your smartphone or tablet:

FREDERICK MCKINLEY JONES

At a mere 14 years of age, R.C. Crothers Garage hired Frederick as a full-time mechanic. Within another year, he became foreman.

Wednesday	Thursday	Friday	Saturday
2	3	4	5
9	10	11	12
16	17	18	19
23	24	25	26
30	31		Post It!

April 2022

S	M	T	W	T	F	S
					1	2
3	4	5	6	7	8	9
10	11	12	13	14	15	16
17	18	19	20	21	22	23
24	25	26	27	28	29	30

March 2022

Work/**LIFE** *Balance*

Meetings

Appointments

Goals

Activities

Meetings

Appointments

Weekly *to-do* List

Monday

Tuesday

Wednesday

Thursday

Friday

Saturday

Sunday

April 2022

Sunday	Monday	Tuesday

Post It!

May 2022

S	M	T	W	T	F	S
1	2	3	4	5	6	7
8	9	10	11	12	13	14
15	16	17	18	19	20	21
22	23	24	25	26	27	28
29	30	31				

3	4	5
10	11	12
17	18	19
24	25	26

MARIAN R. CROAK

Marian R. Croak helped develop a revolutionary communication method that has narrowed the world: VoIP (Voice over Internet Protocol).

Wednesday	Thursday	Friday	Saturday
		1	2
6	7	8	9
13	14	15	16
20	21	22	23
27	28	29	30

April 2022

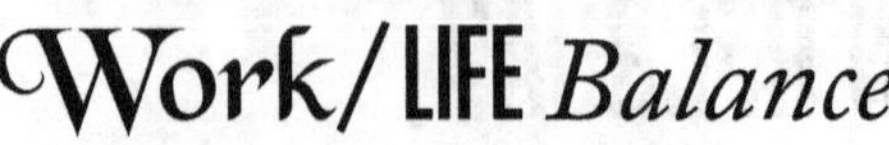

Work/LIFE Balance

Meetings

Appointments

Goals

Activities

Meetings

Appointments

Weekly *to-do* List

<table>
<tr><td>Monday</td><td></td><td rowspan="3">Saturday</td></tr>
<tr><td>Tuesday</td><td></td></tr>
<tr><td>Wednesday</td><td></td></tr>
<tr><td>Thursday</td><td></td><td rowspan="2">Sunday</td></tr>
<tr><td>Friday</td><td></td></tr>
</table>

May 2022

Sunday	Monday	Tuesday
1	2	3
8	9	10
15	16	17
22	23	24
29	30	31

MARIAN R. CROAK

Marian attended Catholic schools until the tenth grade. She switched to a local public school that cultivated her passion for math and science.

Wednesday	Thursday	Friday	Saturday
4	5	6	7
11	12	13	14
18	19	20	21
25	26	27	28

June 2022

S	M	T	W	T	F	S
			1	2	3	4
5	6	7	8	9	10	11
12	13	14	15	16	17	18
19	20	21	22	23	24	25
26	27	28	29	30		

Post It!

Meetings

Appointments

Goals

Activities

Weekly *to-do* List

Monday

Tuesday

Wednesday

Thursday

Friday

Saturday

Sunday

June 2022

Sunday	Monday	Tuesday
5	6	7
12	13	14
19	20	21
26	27	28

MARIAN R. CROAK

Marian held several senior positions with AT&T before leaving the company for Google, where she was hired as vice president of engineering.

Wednesday	Thursday	Friday	Saturday
1	2	3	4
8	9	10	11
15	16	17	18
22	23	24	25
29	30		

July 2022

S	M	T	W	T	F	S
					1	2
3	4	5	6	7	8	9
10	11	12	13	14	15	16
17	18	19	20	21	22	23
24	25	26	27	28	29	30
31						

Post It!

June 2022

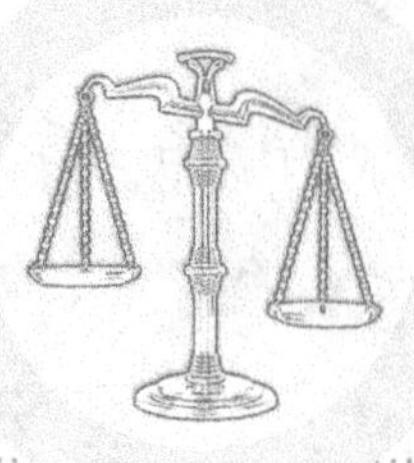

Work/LIFE Balance

Meetings

Appointments

Goals

Activities

Monday

Tuesday

Wednesday

Thursday

Friday

Saturday

Sunday

July 2022

Sunday	Monday	Tuesday

Post It!

August 2022

S	M	T	W	T	F	S
	1	2	3	4	5	6
7	8	9	10	11	12	13
14	15	16	17	18	19	20
21	22	23	24	25	26	27
28	29	30	31			

3	4	5
10	11	12
17	18	19
24	25	26
31		

LEWIS HOWARD LATIMER

Though hardly a household name, black inventor Lewis Howard Latimer influenced the evolution of the marvel that is electric lighting.

Wednesday	Thursday	Friday	Saturday
		1	2
6	7	8	9
13	14	15	16
20	21	22	23
27	28	29	30

July 2022

Work/LIFE Balance

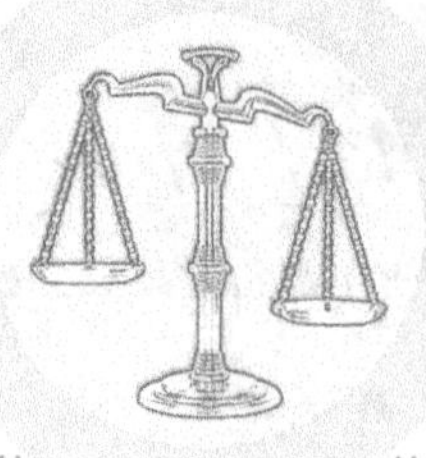

Meetings

Appointments

Goals

Activities

Weekly *to-do* List

August 2022

Sunday	Monday	Tuesday
	1	2
7	8	9
14	15	16
21	22	23
28	29	30

LEWIS HOWARD LATIMER

Lewis immersed himself in mechanical drawing and loved it so much that he used his own money to purchase drafting instruments and books.

Wednesday	Thursday	Friday	Saturday
3	4	5	6
10	11	12	13
17	18	19	20
24	25	26	27
31			

September 2022

S	M	T	W	T	F	S
				1	2	3
4	5	6	7	8	9	10
11	12	13	14	15	16	17
18	19	20	21	22	23	24
25	26	27	28	29	30	

Post It!

August 2022

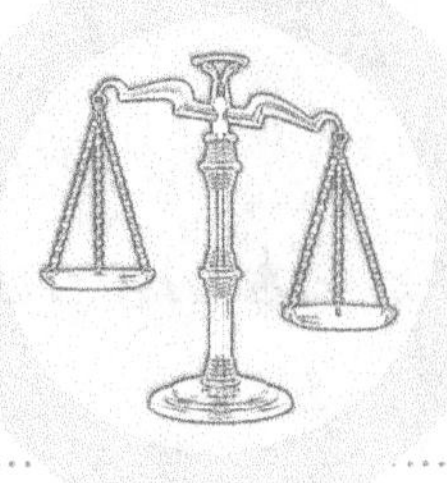

Work/LIFE Balance

Meetings

Appointments

Goals

Activities

Weekly *to-do* List

<table>
<tr><td>

Monday

Tuesday

Wednesday

Thursday

Friday

</td><td>

Saturday

Sunday

</td></tr>
</table>

September 2022

Sunday	Monday	Tuesday
Post It! **INVENTORS**	**October 2022** S M T W T F S 1 2 3 4 5 6 7 8 9 10 11 12 13 14 15 16 17 18 19 20 21 22 23 24 25 26 27 28 29 30 31	
4	5	6
11	12	13
18	19	20
25	26	27

Learn more by scanning the QR code using the camera on your smartphone or tablet:

Lewis successfully improved incandescent lamps by producing a carbon filament that was more durable than the popular variety in wide use.

Wednesday	Thursday	Friday	Saturday
	1	2	3
7	8	9	10
14	15	16	17
21	22	23	24
28	29	30	

September 2022

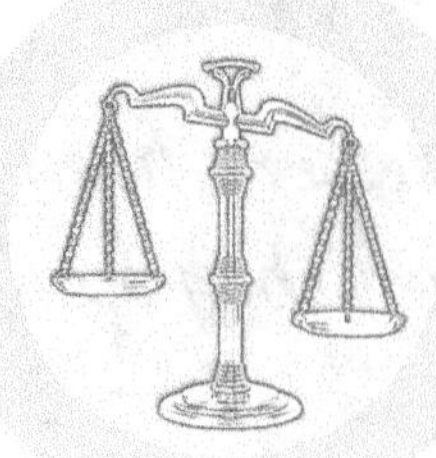

Work/LIFE Balance

Meetings	Appointments

Goals	Activities

Monday

Tuesday

Wednesday

Thursday

Friday

Saturday

Sunday

October 2022

Sunday	Monday	Tuesday

November 2022

S	M	T	W	T	F	S
		1	2	3	4	5
6	7	8	9	10	11	12
13	14	15	16	17	18	19
20	21	22	23	24	25	26
27	28	29	30			

2	3	4

9	10	11

16	17	18

23	24	25

30	31	

MARK DEAN

Mark Dean is a computer engineer who led a creative team in developing the Industry Standard Architecture ecosystem, which expanded the PC.

Wednesday	Thursday	Friday	Saturday
			1
5	6	7	8
12	13	14	15
19	20	21	22
26	27	28	29

October 2022

Work/LIFE Balance

Meetings

Appointments

Goals

Activities

Meetings

Appointments

Weekly *to-do* List

<table>
<tr><td>Monday</td><td></td><td>Saturday</td></tr>
<tr><td>Tuesday</td><td></td><td></td></tr>
<tr><td>Wednesday</td><td></td><td>Sunday</td></tr>
<tr><td>Thursday</td><td></td><td></td></tr>
<tr><td>Friday</td><td></td><td></td></tr>
</table>

November 2022

Sunday	Monday	Tuesday
		1
6	7	8
13	14	15
20	21	22
27	28	29

MARK DEAN

Mark admired his father, James, for his mechanical skills. Together, they successfully rebuilt a 1931 Dodge and a 1947 Chevy.

Wednesday	Thursday	Friday	Saturday
2	3	4	5
9	10	11	12
16	17	18	19
23	24	25	26
30			

December 2022

S	M	T	W	T	F	S
				1	2	3
4	5	6	7	8	9	10
11	12	13	14	15	16	17
18	19	20	21	22	23	24
25	26	27	28	29	30	31

Post It!

November 2022

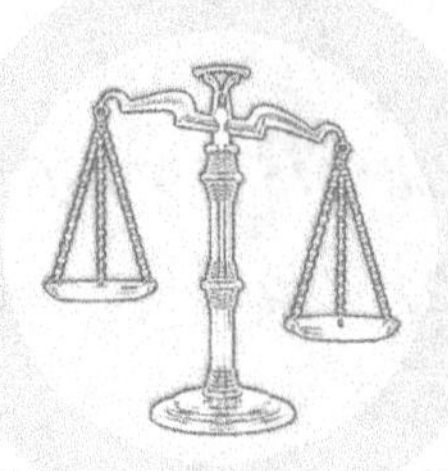

Work/LIFE Balance

Meetings

Appointments

Goals

Activities

Meetings

Appointments

Weekly *to-do* List

Monday

Tuesday

Wednesday

Thursday

Friday

Saturday

Sunday

December 2022

Sunday	Monday	Tuesday

Post It!

January 2023

S	M	T	W	T	F	S
1	2	3	4	5	6	7
8	9	10	11	12	13	14
15	16	17	18	19	20	21
22	23	24	25	26	27	28
29	30	31				

4	5	6
11	12	13
18	19	20
25	26	27

INVENTORS

Learn more by scanning the QR code using the camera on your smartphone or tablet:

MARK DEAN

In the late 1990s, Mark moved to Austin, Texas, to lead an engineering team at IBM's lab in developing the first gigahertz chip.

Wednesday	Thursday	Friday	Saturday
	1	2	3
7	8	9	10
14	15	16	17
21	22	23	24
28	29	30	31

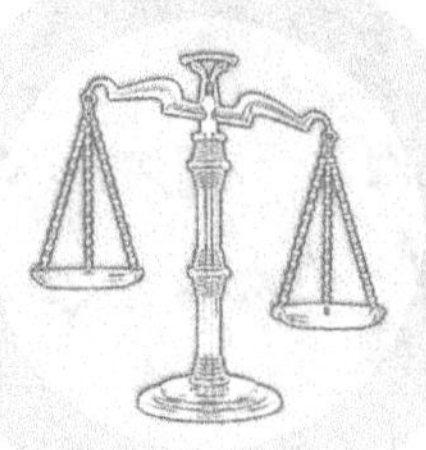

Work/LIFE Balance

Meetings

Appointments

Goals

Activities

Meetings

Appointments

Monday

Tuesday

Wednesday

Thursday

Friday

Saturday

Sunday

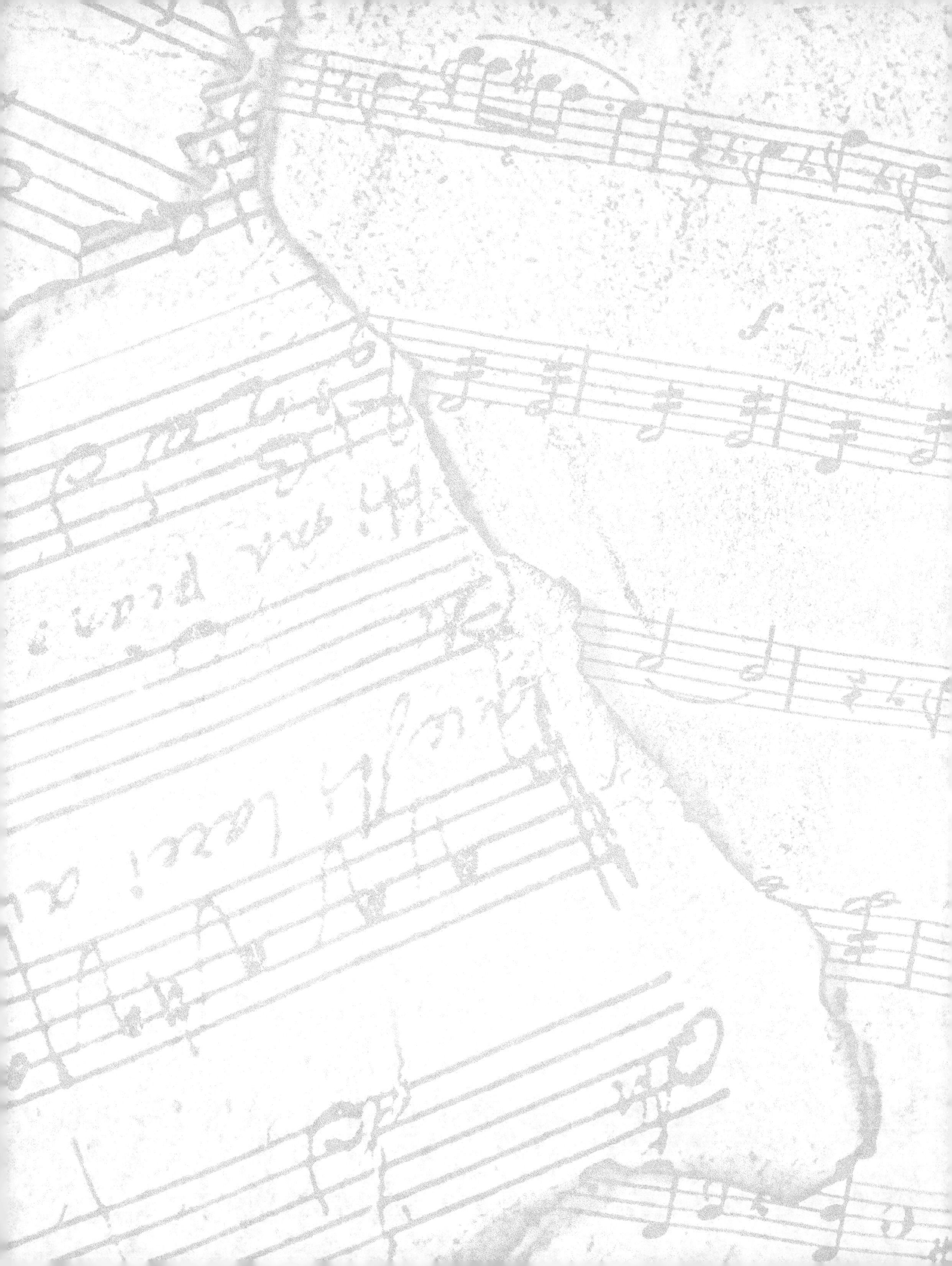

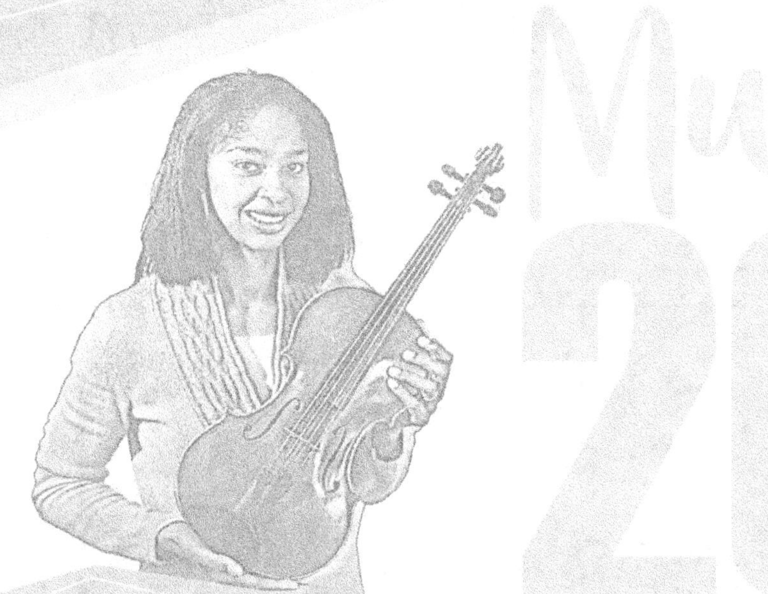

Musicians

2023

"Inspire people around you"

January 2023

Sunday	Monday	Tuesday
1	2	3
8	9	10
15	16	17
22	23	24
29	30	31

After members of the DAR denied Marian access to their stage, she performed at the Lincoln Memorial before an audience of 75,000.

Wednesday	Thursday	Friday	Saturday
4	5	6	7
11	12	13	14
18	19	20	21
25	26	27	28

February 2023

S	M	T	W	T	F	S
			1	2	3	4
5	6	7	8	9	10	11
12	13	14	15	16	17	18
19	20	21	22	23	24	25
26	27	28				

Post It!

January 2023

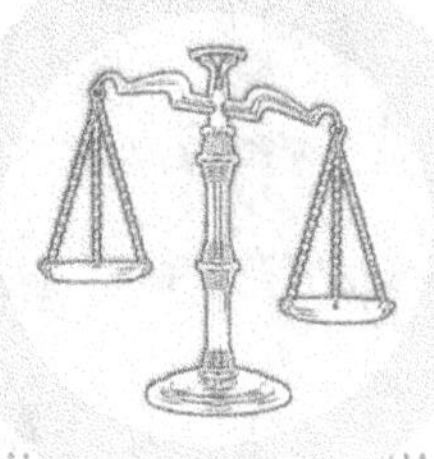

Work/LIFE Balance

Meetings

Appointments

Goals

Activities

Monday

Tuesday

Wednesday

Thursday

Friday

Saturday

Sunday

February 2023

Sunday	Monday	Tuesday
5	6	7
12	13	14
19	20	21
26	27	28

MARIAN ANDERSON

In the early 1920s, Marian toured the United States and traveled through the Jim Crow South by train, all the time enduring racial prejudice.

Wednesday	Thursday	Friday	Saturday
1	2	3	4
8	9	10	11
15	16	17	18
22	23	24	25

March 2023

S	M	T	W	T	F	S
			1	2	3	4
5	6	7	8	9	10	11
12	13	14	15	16	17	18
19	20	21	22	23	24	25
26	27	28	29	30	31	

Post It!

February 2023

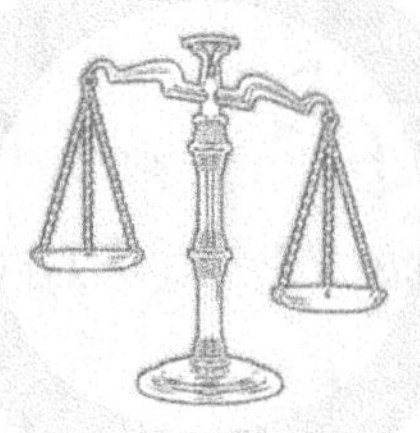

Work/LIFE Balance

Meetings

Appointments

Goals

Activities

Monday

Tuesday

Wednesday

Thursday

Friday

Saturday

Sunday

March 2023

Sunday	Monday	Tuesday

MUSICIANS

Post It!

April 2023

S	M	T	W	T	F	S
						1
2	3	4	5	6	7	8
9	10	11	12	13	14	15
16	17	18	19	20	21	22
23	24	25	26	27	28	29
30						

5	6	7
12	13	14
19	20	21
26	27	28

Learn more by scanning the QR code using the camera on your smartphone or tablet:

MARIAN ANDERSON

But in her career, Marian sang in the presence of presidents and kings and delighted audiences in concert halls and opera houses throughout the world.

Wednesday	Thursday	Friday	Saturday
1	2	3	4
8	9	10	11
15	16	17	18
22	23	24	25
29	30	31	

March 2023

Work/**LIFE** *Balance*

Meetings

Appointments

Goals

Activities

Weekly *to-do* List

<table>
<tr><td>Monday</td><td></td></tr>
<tr><td></td><td>Saturday</td></tr>
<tr><td>Tuesday</td><td></td></tr>
<tr><td>Wednesday</td><td></td></tr>
<tr><td></td><td>Sunday</td></tr>
<tr><td>Thursday</td><td></td></tr>
<tr><td>Friday</td><td></td></tr>
</table>

April 2023

Sunday	Monday	Tuesday
Post It!	**May 2023** S M T W T F S 1 2 3 4 5 6 7 8 9 10 11 12 13 14 15 16 17 18 19 20 21 22 23 24 25 26 27 28 29 30 31	
2	3	4
9	10	11
16	17	18
23 / 30	24	25

JESSYE NORMAN

Jessye Norman gave impressive performances in operas, recitals, and concerts and won multiple Grammy Awards, including one for lifetime achievement.

Wednesday	Thursday	Friday	Saturday
			1
5	6	7	8
12	13	14	15
19	20	21	22
26	27	28	29

April 2023

Work/LIFE Balance

Meetings

Appointments

Goals

Activities

Meetings

Appointments

Monday

Tuesday

Wednesday

Thursday

Friday

Saturday

Sunday

May 2023

Sunday	Monday	Tuesday
	1	2
7	8	9
14	15	16
21	22	23
28	29	30

JESSYE NORMAN

Jessye earned a bachelor's degree in music from Howard University, and she also studied at the University of Michigan and Peabody Institute.

Wednesday	Thursday	Friday	Saturday
3	4	5	6
10	11	12	13
17	18	19	20
24	25	26	27
31			

June 2023

S	M	T	W	T	F	S
				1	2	3
4	5	6	7	8	9	10
11	12	13	14	15	16	17
18	19	20	21	22	23	24
25	26	27	28	29	30	

Post It!

May 2023

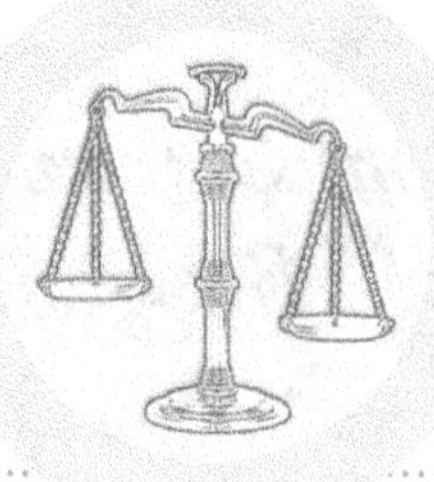

Work/LIFE Balance

Meetings

Appointments

Goals

Activities

Weekly *to-do* List

Monday

Tuesday

Wednesday

Thursday

Friday

Saturday

Sunday

June 2023

Sunday	Monday	Tuesday

Post It!

July 2023

S	M	T	W	T	F	S
						1
2	3	4	5	6	7	8
9	10	11	12	13	14	15
16	17	18	19	20	21	22
23	24	25	26	27	28	29
30	31					

4	5	6
11	12	13
18	19	20
25	26	27

Learn more by scanning the QR code using the camera on your smartphone or tablet:

JESSYE NORMAN

With vocal charisma, Jessye effortlessly sang the classical notes of concert arias fully fleshed, with the graceful accompaniment of the pit orchestra.

Wednesday	Thursday	Friday	Saturday
	1	2	3
7	8	9	10
14	15	16	17
21	22	23	24
28	29	30	

June 2023

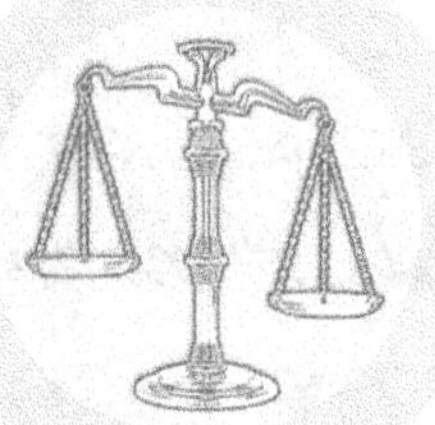

Work/LIFE Balance

Meetings

Appointments

Goals

Activities

Monday

Tuesday

Wednesday

Thursday

Friday

Saturday

Sunday

July 2023

Sunday	Monday	Tuesday
Post It!	**August 2023** S M T W T F S 1 2 3 4 5 6 7 8 9 10 11 12 13 14 15 16 17 18 19 20 21 22 23 24 25 26 27 28 29 30 31	
2	3	4
9	10	11
16	17	18
23 / 30	24 / 31	25

SHEKU KANNEH-MASON

British cellist Sheku Kanneh–Mason earned a measure of notoriety after winning the BBC Young Musician of the Year in 2016.

Wednesday	Thursday	Friday	Saturday
			1
5	6	7	8
12	13	14	15
19	20	21	22
26	27	28	29

July 2023 — Work/LIFE Balance

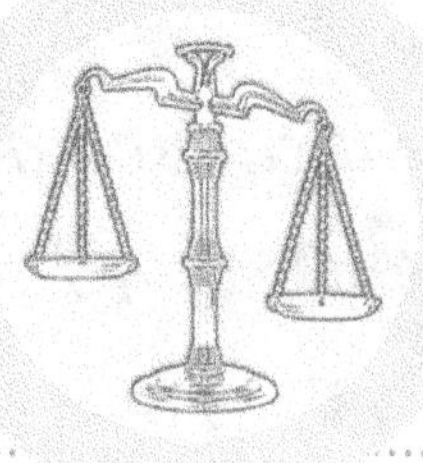

Meetings

Appointments

Goals

Activities

Weekly *to-do* List

August 2023

Sunday	Monday	Tuesday
		1
6	7	8
13	14	15
20	21	22
27	28	29

SHEKU KANNEH-MASON

Then in 2018, Sheku's fame skyrocketed when he played for 600 guests at Prince Harry and Meghan Markle's royal wedding.

Wednesday	Thursday	Friday	Saturday
2	3	4	5
9	10	11	12
16	17	18	19
23	24	25	26
30	31		

September 2023

S	M	T	W	T	F	S
					1	2
3	4	5	6	7	8	9
10	11	12	13	14	15	16
17	18	19	20	21	22	23
24	25	26	27	28	29	30

Post It!

August 2023 — Work/LIFE Balance

Meetings

Appointments

Goals

Activities

Weekly *to-do* List

Monday

Tuesday

Wednesday

Thursday

Friday

Saturday

Sunday

September 2023

Sunday	Monday	Tuesday
Post It!	**October 2023** S M T W T F S 1 2 3 4 5 6 7 8 9 10 11 12 13 14 15 16 17 18 19 20 21 22 23 24 25 26 27 28 29 30 31	
3	4	5
10	11	12
17	18	19
24	25	26

MUSICIANS

SHEKU KANNEH-MASON

Sheku made history again in 2020 when his album Elgar landed in the Top 10 of the UK Official Album Chart, making him the first cellist to do so.

Wednesday	Thursday	Friday	Saturday
		1	2
6	7	8	9
13	14	15	16
20	21	22	23
27	28	29	30

September 2023 — Work/LIFE Balance

Meetings

Appointments

Goals

Activities

Weekly *to-do* List

October 2023

Sunday	Monday	Tuesday
1	2	3
8	9	10
15	16	17
22	23	24
29	30	31

GINGER SMOCK

Ginger Smock paved the way for other talented female musicians with her blues-infused violin solos that carried harmonic structures akin to the horn.

Wednesday	Thursday	Friday	Saturday
4	5	6	7
11	12	13	14
18	19	20	21
25	26	27	28

November 2023

S	M	T	W	T	F	S
			1	2	3	4
5	6	7	8	9	10	11
12	13	14	15	16	17	18
19	20	21	22	23	24	25
26	27	28	29	30		

Post It!

October 2023

Work/LIFE Balance

Meetings	Appointments

Goals	Activities

Weekly *to-do* List

Monday

Tuesday

Wednesday

Thursday

Friday

Saturday

Sunday

November 2023

Sunday	Monday	Tuesday
5	6	7
12	13	14
19	20	21
26	27	28

GINGER SMOCK

Ginger proved to be a prodigy. A rare performance she gave at the Hollywood Bowl at age ten resulted in a standing ovation.

Wednesday	Thursday	Friday	Saturday
1	2	3	4
8	9	10	11
15	16	17	18
22	23	24	25
29	30		Post It!

December 2023

S	M	T	W	T	F	S
					1	2
3	4	5	6	7	8	9
10	11	12	13	14	15	16
17	18	19	20	21	22	23
24	25	26	27	28	29	30
31						

November 2023

Work/LIFE Balance

Meetings	Appointments

Goals	Activities

Weekly *to-do* List

Monday

Tuesday

Wednesday

Thursday

Friday

Saturday

Sunday

December 2023

Sunday	Monday	Tuesday

Post It!

January 2024

S	M	T	W	T	F	S
	1	2	3	4	5	6
7	8	9	10	11	12	13
14	15	16	17	18	19	20
21	22	23	24	25	26	27
28	29	30	31			

3	4	5
10	11	12
17	18	19
24	25	26
31		

Learn more by scanning the QR code using the camera on your smartphone or tablet:

▼

GINGER SMOCK

Ginger made her television debut in 1951 when she hosted a thirty-minute TV show that aired on CBS affiliate KTSL for six weeks.

Wednesday	Thursday	Friday	Saturday
		1	2
6	7	8	9
13	14	15	16
20	21	22	23
27	28	29	30

December 2023 — Work/LIFE Balance

Meetings

Appointments

Goals

Activities

Weekly *to-do* List

Monday

Tuesday

Wednesday

Thursday

Friday

Saturday

Sunday

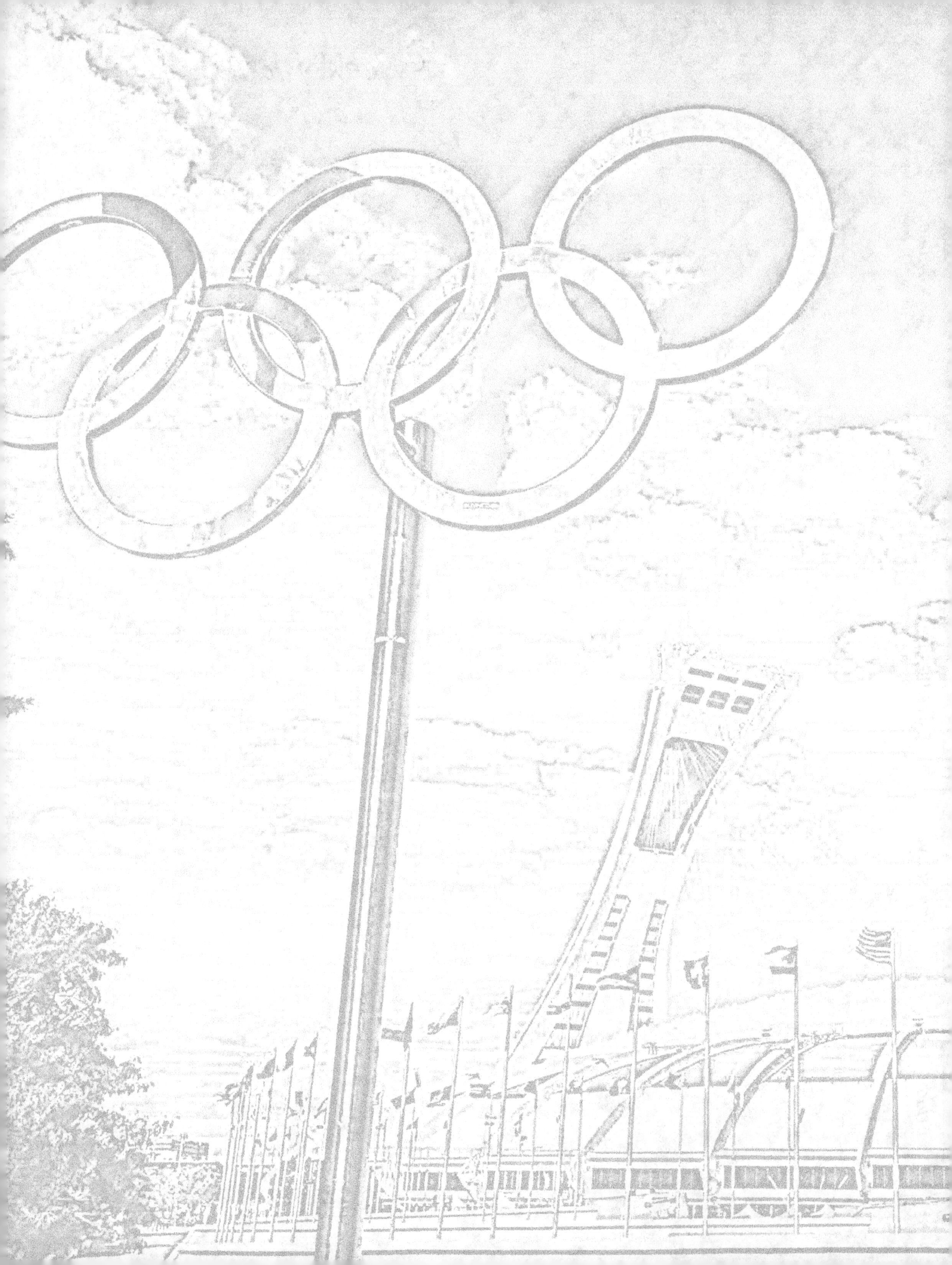

Olympians
2024
"Victory awaits you"

January 2024

Sunday	Monday	Tuesday
	1	2
7	8	9
14	15	16
21	22	23
28	29	30

SIMONE BILES

Simone Biles, the most decorated gymnast in U.S. history, has been shattering records since her entrance into the world of professional gymnastics.

Wednesday	Thursday	Friday	Saturday
3	4	5	6
10	11	12	13
17	18	19	20
24	25	26	27
31			

February 2024

S	M	T	W	T	F	S
				1	2	3
4	5	6	7	8	9	10
11	12	13	14	15	16	17
18	19	20	21	22	23	24
25	26	27	28	29		

Post It!

January 2024

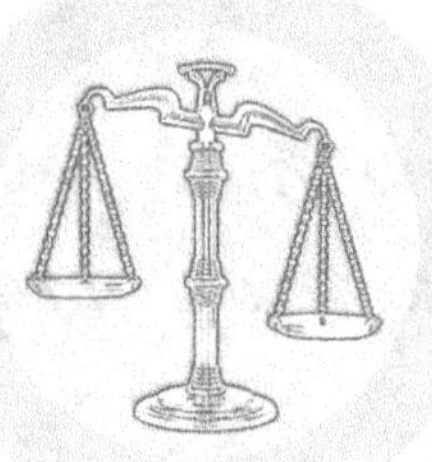

Work/LIFE Balance

Meetings

Appointments

Goals

Activities

Meetings

Appointments

Weekly *to-do* List

Monday

Tuesday

Wednesday

Thursday

Friday

Saturday

Sunday

February 2024

Sunday	Monday	Tuesday
4	5	6
11	12	13
18	19	20
25	26	27

SIMONE BILES

Simone is also the first woman to win three consecutive all-around titles in the history of World Gymnastics and has won the most world medals.

Wednesday	Thursday	Friday	Saturday
	1	2	3
7	8	9	10
14	15	16	17
21	22	23	24
28	29		Post It!

March 2024

S	M	T	W	T	F	S
					1	2
3	4	5	6	7	8	9
10	11	12	13	14	15	16
17	18	19	20	21	22	23
24	25	26	27	28	29	30
31						

February 2024

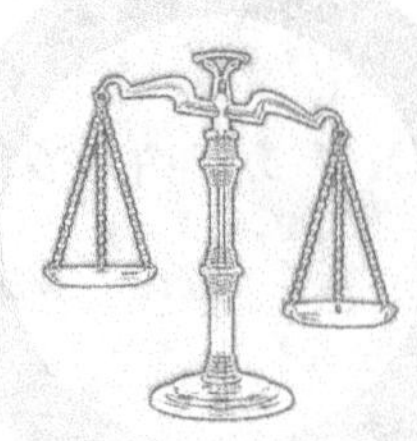

Work/LIFE Balance

Meetings

Appointments

Goals

Activities

Weekly *to-do* List

Monday

Tuesday

Wednesday

Thursday

Friday

Saturday

Sunday

March 2024

Sunday	Monday	Tuesday

Post It!

April 2024

S	M	T	W	T	F	S
	1	2	3	4	5	6
7	8	9	10	11	12	13
14	15	16	17	18	19	20
21	22	23	24	25	26	27
28	29	30				

3	4	5
10	11	12
17	18	19
24	25	26
31		

Learn more by scanning the QR code using the camera on your smartphone or tablet:

SIMONE BILES

Simone is distinguished for the complexity she incorporates into her routines, be it uneven bars, vault, balance beam, or floor exercise.

Wednesday	Thursday	Friday	Saturday
		1	2
6	7	8	9
13	14	15	16
20	21	22	23
27	28	29	30

Work/LIFE Balance

Meetings

Appointments

Goals

Activities

Weekly *to-do* List

Monday

Tuesday

Wednesday

Thursday

Friday

Saturday

Sunday

April 2024

Sunday	Monday	Tuesday
	1	2
7	8	9
14	15	16
21	22	23
28	29	30

MARITZA CORREIA McCLENDON

Maritza Correia McClendon made history as the first black woman to qualify for a spot on the U.S. Olympic Swim Team and win a medal.

Wednesday	Thursday	Friday	Saturday
3	4	5	6
10	11	12	13
17	18	19	20
24	25	26	27

May 2024

S	M	T	W	T	F	S
			1	2	3	4
5	6	7	8	9	10	11
12	13	14	15	16	17	18
19	20	21	22	23	24	25
26	27	28	29	30	31	

Post It!

April 2024

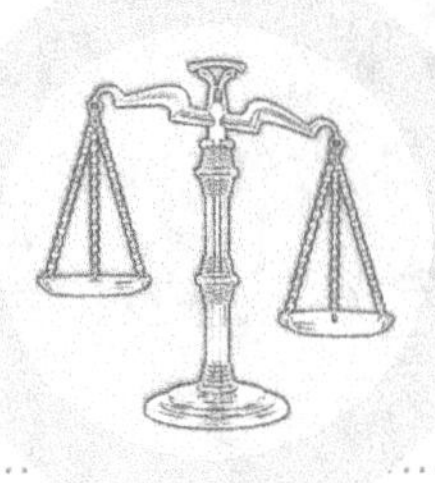

Work/LIFE Balance

Meetings

Appointments

Goals

Activities

Weekly *to-do* List

Monday

Tuesday

Wednesday

Thursday

Friday

Saturday

Sunday

May 2024

Sunday	Monday	Tuesday

June 2024

S	M	T	W	T	F	S
						1
2	3	4	5	6	7	8
9	10	11	12	13	14	15
16	17	18	19	20	21	22
23	24	25	26	27	28	29
30						

5	6	7
12	**13**	**14**
19	**20**	**21**
26	**27**	**28**

MARITZA CORREIA McCLENDON

Maritza joined the swim team at Tampa Bay Technical High. In her senior year, she became a U.S. national champion for the 50-meter freestyle.

Wednesday	Thursday	Friday	Saturday
1	2	3	4
8	9	10	11
15	16	17	18
22	23	24	25
29	30	31	

May 2024

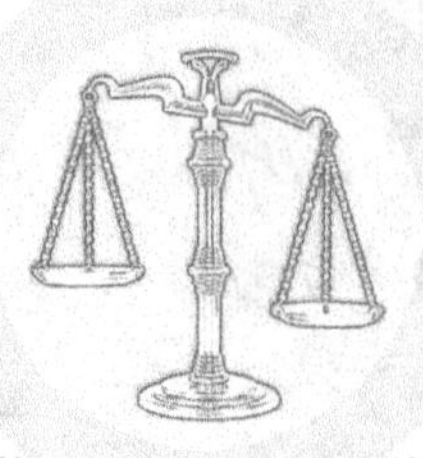

Work/LIFE Balance

Meetings

Appointments

Goals

Activities

Meetings

Appointments

Weekly *to-do* List

Monday

Tuesday

Wednesday

Thursday

Friday

Saturday

Sunday

June 2024

Sunday	Monday	Tuesday

Post It!

July 2024

S	M	T	W	T	F	S
	1	2	3	4	5	6
7	8	9	10	11	12	13
14	15	16	17	18	19	20
21	22	23	24	25	26	27
28	29	30	31			

2	3	4
9	10	11
16	17	18
23	24	25
30		

Learn more by scanning the QR code using the camera on your smartphone or tablet:

MARITZA CORREIA McCLENDON

Before graduating college in 2005, Maritza became a 27-time All-American and one of the most decorated swimmers in the history of the NCAA.

Wednesday	Thursday	Friday	Saturday
			1
5	6	7	8
12	13	14	15
19	20	21	22
26	27	28	29

June 2024

Work/LIFE Balance

Meetings

Appointments

Goals

Activities

Weekly *to-do* List

July 2024

Sunday	Monday	Tuesday
	1	2
7	8	9
14	15	16
21	22	23
28	29	30

TAMYRA MENSAH-STOCK

Wrestler Tamyra Mensah-Stock is the first black woman to win an Olympic gold medal for the United States. She cried tears of joy upon making history.

Wednesday	Thursday	Friday	Saturday
3	4	5	6
10	11	12	13
17	18	19	20
24	25	26	27
31		August 2024	Post It!

August 2024

S	M	T	W	T	F	S
				1	2	3
4	5	6	7	8	9	10
11	12	13	14	15	16	17
18	19	20	21	22	23	24
25	26	27	28	29	30	31

July 2024

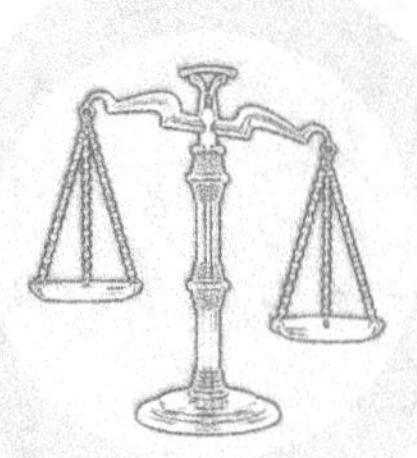

Work/LIFE Balance

Meetings

Appointments

Goals

Activities

Meetings

Appointments

Weekly *to-do* List

Monday

Tuesday

Wednesday

Thursday

Friday

Saturday

Sunday

August 2024

Sunday	Monday	Tuesday
Post It!	**September 2024** S M T W T F S 1 2 3 4 5 6 7 8 9 10 11 12 13 14 15 16 17 18 19 20 21 22 23 24 25 26 27 28 29 30	
4	5	6
11	12	13
18	19	20
25	26	27

TAMYRA MENSAH-STOCK

As a professional wrestler, Tamyra has traveled the world to compete, but of her own country, she fondly stated: "I love representing the U.S."

Wednesday	Thursday	Friday	Saturday
	1	2	3
7	8	9	10
14	15	16	17
21	22	23	24
28	29	30	31

August 2024

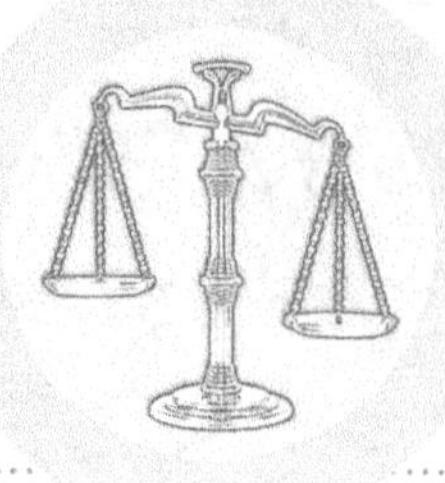

Work/LIFE Balance

Meetings

Appointments

Goals

Activities

Monday

Tuesday

Wednesday

Thursday

Friday

Saturday

Sunday

September 2024

Sunday	Monday	Tuesday
1	2	3
8	9	10
15	16	17
22	23	24
29	30	

Learn more by scanning the QR code using the camera on your smartphone or tablet:

TAMYRA MENSAH-STOCK

Tamyra planned to use a portion of her Olympic prize money to buy a food truck for her mother, but Cruising Kitchens gifted her with a $250,000 truck.

Wednesday	Thursday	Friday	Saturday
4	5	6	7
11	12	13	14
18	19	20	21
25	26	27	28

October 2024

S	M	T	W	T	F	S
		1	2	3	4	5
6	7	8	9	10	11	12
13	14	15	16	17	18	19
20	21	22	23	24	25	26
27	28	29	30	31		

Post It!

September 2024

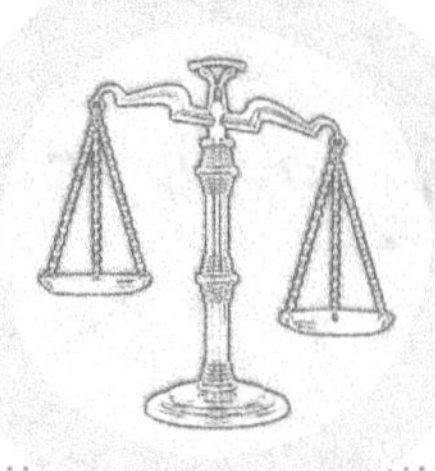

Work/LIFE Balance

Meetings

Appointments

Goals

Activities

Meetings

Monday

Tuesday

Wednesday

Thursday

Friday

Saturday

Sunday

October 2024

Sunday	Monday	Tuesday
		1
6	7	8
13	14	15
20	21	22
27	28	29

USAIN BOLT

Jamaican Usain Bolt became a living legend and was declared "the fastest man alive" after breaking world records and winning several Olympic gold medals.

Wednesday	Thursday	Friday	Saturday
2	3	4	5
9	10	11	12
16	17	18	19
23	24	25	26
30	31		*Post It!*

November 2024

S	M	T	W	T	F	S
					1	2
3	4	5	6	7	8	9
10	11	12	13	14	15	16
17	18	19	20	21	22	23
24	25	26	27	28	29	30

October 2024

Work/**LIFE** Balance

Meetings

Appointments

Goals

Activities

Meetings

Weekly *to-do* List

<table>
<tr><td>Monday</td><td></td></tr>
<tr><td></td><td>Saturday</td></tr>
<tr><td>Tuesday</td><td></td></tr>
<tr><td>Wednesday</td><td></td></tr>
<tr><td></td><td>Sunday</td></tr>
<tr><td>Thursday</td><td></td></tr>
<tr><td>Friday</td><td></td></tr>
</table>

Sunday	Monday	Tuesday
Post It!	**December 2024** S M T W T F S 1 2 3 4 5 6 7 8 9 10 11 12 13 14 15 16 17 18 19 20 21 22 23 24 25 26 27 28 29 30 31	
3	4	5
10	11	12
17	18	19
24	25	26

Usain was the first to compete in consecutive Olympic games and win the 100- and 200-meter race in both. Another first was winning gold for those races.

Wednesday	Thursday	Friday	Saturday
		1	2
6	7	8	9
13	14	15	16
20	21	22	23
27	28	29	30

November 2024

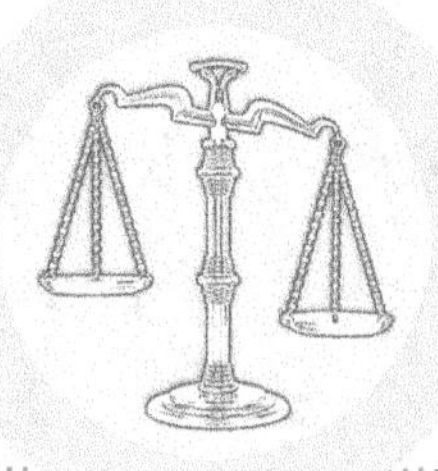

Work/LIFE Balance

Meetings

Appointments

Goals

Activities

Weekly *to-do* List

Monday

Tuesday

Wednesday

Thursday

Friday

Saturday

Sunday

December 2024

Sunday	Monday	Tuesday
1	2	3
8	9	10
15	16	17
22	23	24
29	30	31

OLYMPIANS

Learn more by scanning the QR code using the camera on your smartphone or tablet:

USAIN BOLT

After Usain retired from track and field, he played professional soccer with the Central Coast Mariners of the A-League, a top-flight team in Australia.

Wednesday	Thursday	Friday	Saturday
4	5	6	7
11	12	13	14
18	19	20	21
25	26	27	28

January 2025

S	M	T	W	T	F	S
			1	2	3	4
5	6	7	8	9	10	11
12	13	14	15	16	17	18
19	20	21	22	23	24	25
26	27	28	29	30	31	

Post It!

December 2024

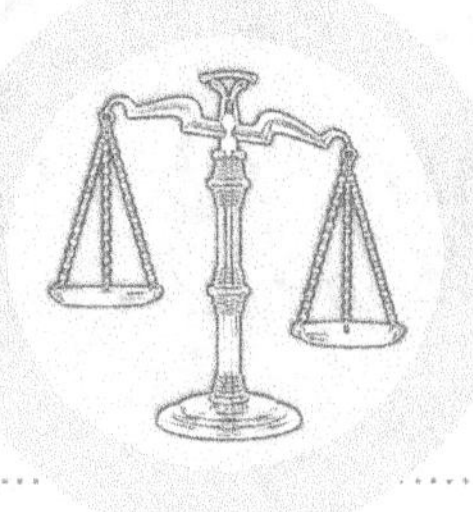

Work/LIFE Balance

Meetings

Appointments

Goals

Activities

Meetings

Appointments

Weekly *to-do* List

Monday

Tuesday

Wednesday

Thursday

Friday

Saturday

Sunday

JOT IT DOWN

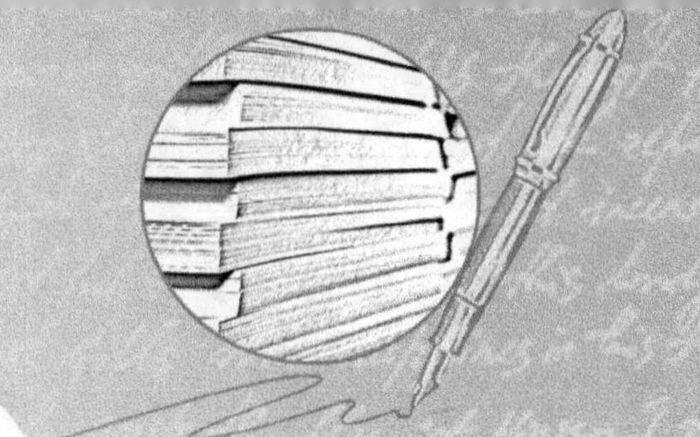

Descriptor	Detail

Descriptor	Detail

Descriptor	Detail

Descriptor	Detail

Descriptor	Detail

Descriptor	Detail

Other Important Items

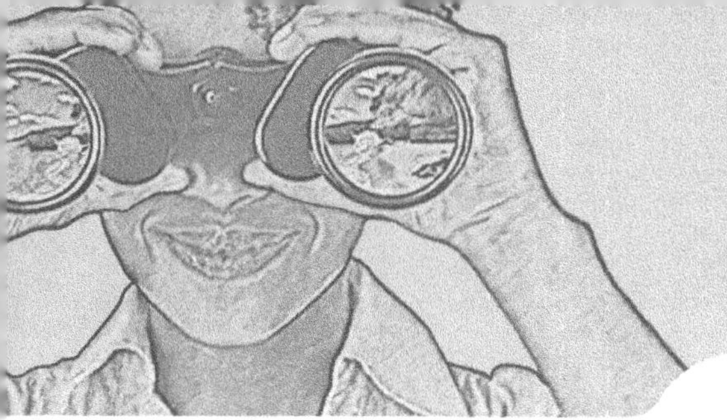

January 2025

S	M	T	W	T	F	S
			1	2	3	4
5	6	7	8	9	10	11
12	13	14	15	16	17	18
19	20	21	22	23	24	25
26	27	28	29	30	31	

February 2025

S	M	T	W	T	F	S
						1
2	3	4	5	6	7	8
9	10	11	12	13	14	15
16	17	18	19	20	21	22
23	24	25	26	27	28	

March 2025

S	M	T	W	T	F	S
						1
2	3	4	5	6	7	8
9	10	11	12	13	14	15
16	17	18	19	20	21	22
23	24	25	26	27	28	29
30	31					

April 2025

S	M	T	W	T	F	S
		1	2	3	4	5
6	7	8	9	10	11	12
13	14	15	16	17	18	19
20	21	22	23	24	25	26
27	28	29	30			

May 2025

S	M	T	W	T	F	S
				1	2	3
4	5	6	7	8	9	10
11	12	13	14	15	16	17
18	19	20	21	22	23	24
25	26	27	28	29	30	31

June 2025

S	M	T	W	T	F	S
1	2	3	4	5	6	7
8	9	10	11	12	13	14
15	16	17	18	19	20	21
22	23	24	25	26	27	28
29	30					

July 2025

S	M	T	W	T	F	S
		1	2	3	4	5
6	7	8	9	10	11	12
13	14	15	16	17	18	19
20	21	22	23	24	25	26
27	28	29	30	31		

August 2025

S	M	T	W	T	F	S
					1	2
3	4	5	6	7	8	9
10	11	12	13	14	15	16
17	18	19	20	21	22	23
24	25	26	27	28	29	30
31						

September 2025

S	M	T	W	T	F	S
	1	2	3	4	5	6
7	8	9	10	11	12	13
14	15	16	17	18	19	20
21	22	23	24	25	26	27
28	29	30				

October 2025

S	M	T	W	T	F	S
			1	2	3	4
5	6	7	8	9	10	11
12	13	14	15	16	17	18
19	20	21	22	23	24	25
26	27	28	29	30	31	

November 2025

S	M	T	W	T	F	S
						1
2	3	4	5	6	7	8
9	10	11	12	13	14	15
16	17	18	19	20	21	22
23	24	25	26	27	28	29
30						

December 2025

S	M	T	W	T	F	S
	1	2	3	4	5	6
7	8	9	10	11	12	13
14	15	16	17	18	19	20
21	22	23	24	25	26	27
28	29	30	31			

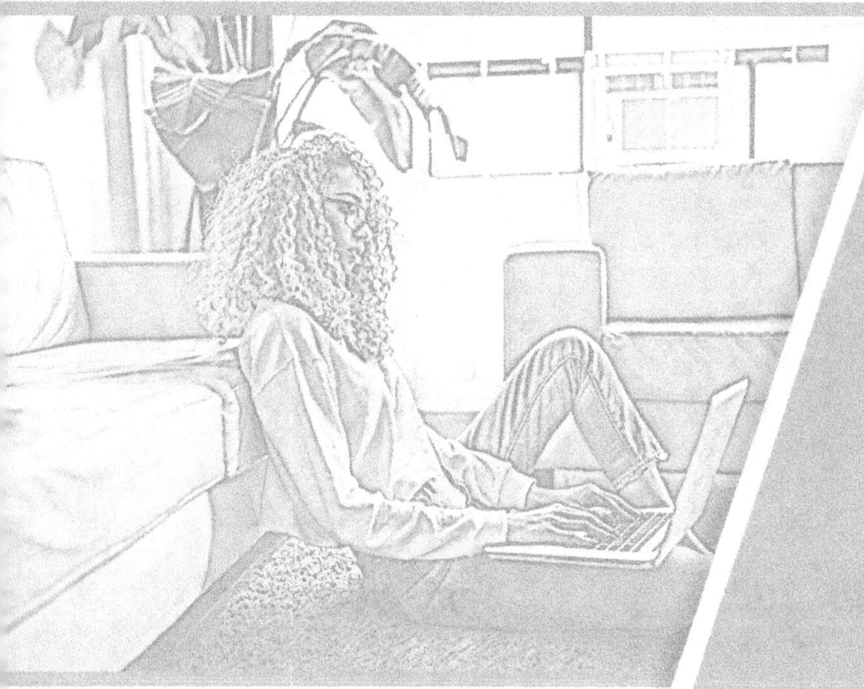

NEWSLETTER

Sign up for our newsletter and immerse yourself in hidden black history.

Scan the QR code using the camera on your smartphone or tablet and . . .

STAY INFORMED